Pre-race preparation: (from left) WR Baird (Riley No 24) and HC McFerran (Bugatti No 10), give instructions to Baird's mechanic. As it turned out, Baird was a non-starter in the 1934 race on medical advice.

THE BRAY MOTOR RACES 1934-1935

Robin McCullagh

Dreoilín

FOREWORD

As a resident of Bray, I am delighted that the latest publication in the Irish Transport Series features the Bray Motor Races 1934 – 1935. This event has had a very low profile in terms of its history. The problem for most who delved into the records was trying to find anything at all that recorded these significant events. It is to Robin McCullagh's enormous credit that firstly, he has taken on the task at all and secondly, that he has succeeded in finding such a collection of photographs and detailed information to make the whole project worthwhile.

The circuit as described is virtually unaltered from its original layout and I would encourage readers of this album to visit Bray and see for themselves exactly the challenges faced by the drivers of the period. The most obvious feature of the venue was the mile long straight that ran along the seafront. However, the circuit designers clearly had great fun plotting the rest of the circuit. I can only guess what it must have been like to try to stop a competition car at the bottom of the Vevay Road in order to take the hairpin back up Killarney Road away from the Town. My suspicion is that many cars would have overshot the course at this point, resulting in an unscheduled visit to Main Street!

The period covered by this album is a very significant time in Irish motorsport, when imaginative organisers were contemplating a range of street races in order to bring the sport to the people. This they succeeded in doing despite the loss of the Grand Prix series in Phoenix Park and the Bray event was an important "toe in the water" in this regard.

My congratulations go to Robin McCullagh on producing such a range of interesting material and to Bob Montgomery, my best thanks for going to the trouble of producing this important addition to the Dreoilín Album series.

Alex Sinclair
Chief Executive
Motorsport Ireland

Front Cover: The Riley of T O'Shaughnessy leads the Statham-Ford Special of M J Hynes in the 1934 race.

HD Walsh (MG No 18), takes Duncairn corner followed by JF Sutherland (Singer No 5). Note how little protection is on the lamp post, and how close to the track the spectators are standing.

IRISH MOTORSPORT IN THE 1930's

Motor Sport in Ireland experienced several highs and lows during the early years of the twentieth century. The highs would include such events as the 1903 'Automobile Fortnight in Ireland', which included the Gordon Bennett Race and the Phoenix Park Speed Trials. Also of importance were the series of Irish International Grand Prix held from 1929-31 in Dublin's Phoenix Park. These Grand Prix were organized by the Royal Irish Automobile Club and only made possible with financial support from the Government of the day.

The low arrived in 1932 with the election of the Fianna Fail party to power for the first time. They decided that they were not going to give any support to what they perceived as a rich man's sport, thus ending any chance of Ireland hosting motor sport events at Grand Prix level for the foreseeable future. Those interested in Motor Sport however continued to seek out ways to indulge their hobby, and during 1932 the Irish Motor Racing Club held races in the Phoenix Park on a National Event basis. The same Club in later years organized round-the-houses races in Bray, Limerick and Cork. The races at Tallaght in County Dublin were organized by the Leinster Motor Club.

BRAY 1934
THE ORGANISING

In 1934, the seaside town of Bray was administrated by a Commissioner and he, along with the towns traders and hoteliers saw merit in holding a motor race as a means of encouraging additional visitors to their town. After all, this was a formula that had already been tried and proven successful in the Isle of Man and on the Continent.

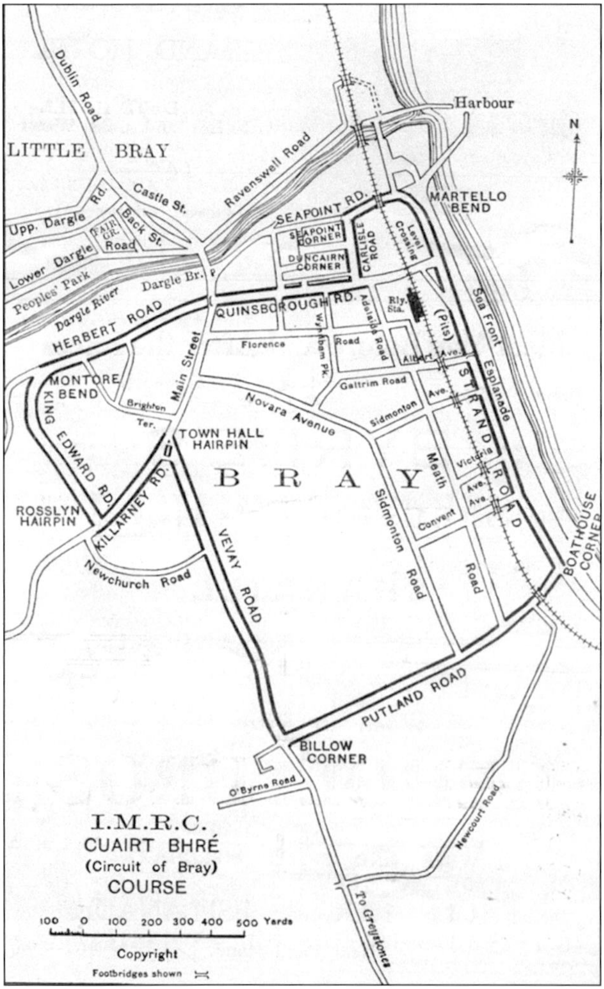

This was the first round-the-houses event in these islands, although five years previously the towns of Comber and Newtownards in Northern Ireland had both seen cars roaring through their streets being driven in anger, that particular course had much more of a rural aspect to it, while Bray was a true urban track. The title chosen for the event, 'Cuairt Bhre', translated as 'Visit Bray'.

Many of Bray's residents were less than happy about being awoken on the Thursday preceding the race by the cars during early morning practice (5 am to 7 am). Engines reverberated from the buildings and the smell of hot racing oil hung in the air and penetrated everything. One elderly woman was heard to say "if they must practice, why don't they go somewhere else to do it!" There was also the problem of restricted movement around their own town on race day, despite the fact that the organisers had provided two temporary pedestrian bridges at critical locations to allow access across the track.

The running of the event was entrusted to the Irish Motor Racing Club (IMRC). Some people believed the task would be beyond the capabilities of a club that had only been in existence for four years. Thankfully those pessimists were proved wrong, with the IMRC gaining nothing but high praise for their marvelous organization of the event.

MJ Hynes (Statham-Ford No 17) overtakes JF Sutherland (Singer No 5)) as they round Vevey Road corner. The steepness of the drop down Vevey Road can be seen in the background.

THE BRAY COURSE

The Start/Finish line was located on the mile long **Strand Road** (Sea Front). The actual pits and starting line were outside the Fitzwilliam Nursing Home with the crowds standing many deep (not far from where the Beach House/Coast Café stand today). From here the cars traveled in a clockwise direction, turning sharp right at **Boathouse Corner** into Putland Road. The continuation of Strand Road (towards the Bray Head Hotel) was used as an escape road. Because of the narrowness of this section of the road passing was forbidden from the corner until the cars had gone under the Railway Bridge.

Putland Road was an up-hill climb of about half a mile with an average gradient of 1 in 20, and brought the cars up to another sharp right turn at **Billow Corner,** so named because the house at the side of the lane opposite the turn (used as an escape road) was called Billow House. (Some ten years later the Queen of Peace Church would be built to the left of this corner).

Having turned right the cars followed **Vevey Road,** flat and twisty at first, and then a severe drop down-hill (gradient 1 in 50) for just over half a mile to the very tight left turn at **Town Hall Hairpin,** into Killarney Road. Bray Main Street was used as an escape road for this corner.

Killarney Road was a short fast uphill stretch to the deceptive and tricky to negotiate **Rosslyn Hairpin** into King Edward Road. **King Edward Road** was down-hill, not very pronounced at first, but becoming accentuated to perhaps 1 in 15 as it reached **Montore Bend,** the right hand bend that leads into Herbert Road.

Herbert Road was two thirds level then wound its way down-hill (gradient of about 1 in 35) to the intersection with Main Street and continued into **Quinsborough Road.** In those days there were no ramps or traffic calming devices as there are today along Quinsborough Road. Another left-hand turn was taken at **Duncairn Corner** into Carlisle Road.

Carlisle Road (also known as **Seymour Road**) was another short stretch before turning right at the obtuse-angled **Seapoint Corner.** Again, from this corner until the drivers went under the Railway Bridge, there was no passing allowed. From the Railway Bridge there was a sharp drop (gradient exceeding 1 in 20) for most of **Seapoint Road** before the road went uphill once more to **Martello Bend** at which point the cars turned right, back onto Strand Road. This gave a total lap distance of 3.2 miles.

Cars racing down Vevey Road towards Town Hall corner. Again the steepness of the hill is evident.

RACE DAY 1934

Race Day, Saturday 19th May 1934 (Whitsun Weekend), dawned dry, bright, and mild, in fact, just perfect racing conditions. All reports talked about buses and trains arriving in the town full. Estimates of crowd numbers differ greatly, with one UK newspaper claiming a figure of 80,000 spectators. Crowd control proved a difficult task for the marshals, as many of the more enthusiastic - and foolhardy - spectators insisted on moving from the footpaths out onto the roadways, particularly at the more difficult to negotiate corners.

THE RACE

In handicap races it is often difficult for the spectators to identify who exactly is doing well and who the eventual winner is likely to be, but from early on in this 32 lap race it was obvious that Ulster driver Trevor McCalla in his supercharged Sunbeam was the fastest man on the track. The big question on everyone's mind was, could he catch the limit-man Dubliner Paddy Le Fanu before the end of the race?

Le Fanu, better known for his exploits in motorcycle competitions, was driving his Adler Trumpf faultlessly. This car, with its front-wheel-drive and excellent handling appeared ideally suited to the tight and many cornered Bray track. All round the circuit the spectators were enthralled by the skill of the drivers, with skids, slides, and liberal use of the escape roads all becoming more plentiful as brakes wore down and driver's enthusiasm increased.

JK Sutherland's Singer (No 5) suffers a massive slide while rounding Boat-house corner during the 1934 race.

By lap eight although consistently lapping at 54 mph McCalla hadn't yet featured on the leader board, as the positions were:-

1st	RBS Le Fanu	Adler
2nd	JF Sutherland	Singer
3rd	G White	MG
4th	HD Walsh	MG
5th	F O'Boyle	Riley
6th	CH Wilson	Vauxhall

McCalla continued his relentless pursuit, his electric horn shrieking to warn the slower drivers of his intension to pass them. Several cars were at this stage forced to call into the pits for adjustments or repairs, some unfortunately finding their problems terminal. Other drivers forcing their way speedily through the field were the Bugatti of HC McFerran and the Statham-Ford of MJ Hynes.

The eventual 1934 race winner, RBS Le Fanu (Adler No 4), rounds the infamous Monument steps at Town Hall corner.

On lap sixteen the positions were:-

1st	Le Fanu	Adler
2nd	O'Boyle	Riley
3rd	Sutherland	Singer
4th	White	MG
5th	WT McCalla	Sunbeam
6th	MJ Hynes	Statham-Ford

On lap nineteen McCalla, Union Flags emblazoned on the sides of the big Sunbeam's bonnet, had cut the original handicap of 4 laps and 1 minute to Le Fanu down by nearly three laps, and he was far from finished yet, keeping the pressure on in his pursuit of the limit-man.

O'Boyle, Wilson, and Hynes, were all forced to retire with mechanical difficulties, while McFerran drove on despite having earlier had a close encounter with a wall and injuring his wrist in the process. Then, at Martello Bend he skidded on the slightly loose surface and crashed into the wall, finishing that lap on foot. Once again there were changes to the configuration of the leader board and on lap twenty-four it now read:-

On lap twenty-four the positions were:-

1st	Le Fanu	Adler
2nd	McCalla	Sunbeam
3rd	Neill	Bugatti.
4th	White	MG

CG Neill (Bugatti No 16), was fortunate to survive when his car skidded, hit a bank, and somersaulted three times.

With eight laps to go McCalla had cut the time between himself and Le Fanu down to 2 minutes 23 seconds. Then on lap twenty-six near disaster struck McCalla. Firstly his pit crew held up a board with 4 on it, meaning four laps to go, but their driver thought they meant that he should keep the engine revs below 4000 and slowed down accordingly. Then he overshot the Town Hall Hairpin losing valuable seconds while he reversed up Bray Main Street to get back on track. Finally, he got battery acid in his eyes, splashed up from the battery which was sitting where normally the passenger seat would have been. Drivers of this caliber are made of stern stuff however, and it wasn't long before our hero was back again in full flight and hunting down his prey.

Going into the final lap the gap between McCalla and Le Fanu was down to just 37 seconds, and it looked possible for the County Down man to take the spoils. However, in his exuberance he squandered valuable seconds with several speed-sapping slides on some of the corners. With the crowd on their toes with excitement and the noise at crescendo pitch, this final lap appeared to last for an eternity, although perhaps, from their cockpits the drivers saw things differently. When Le Fanu crossed the finish line to take the chequered flag, he was only slowing down when second placed man McCalla caught up with him. The gap between the two of them at the line was a mere 2.35 seconds, thus indicating that the handicappers had made some just about spot-on calculations. Le Fanu's average speed for the race was 45.5 mph, while McCalla's was 52.62 mph.

Second placed driver W T McCalla (Sunbeam No 9), is congratulated by CG Neill and HC McFerran, both of whom had crashed Bugatti's during the race.

1934 RACE
LIST OF CARS, DRIVERS AND RACE RESULT.

1. C W Taylor, Le Mans Singer 972cc - car entered by PJ Tracy Ltd. Finished 4th. Awarded the Dennis Feighery Cup (presented by Mr. D Feighery of the South of Ireland Asphalt Company) – to be won outright + £10*.

2. D McMullan, MG Magnette 1287cc. Retired with mechanical trouble.

3. C H Wilson, Vauxhall 4226cc. Retired with mechanical trouble.

4. R B S Le Fanu, Adler 1994cc. Finished 1st, Awarded the Earl of Meath's Trophy, (perpetual) with Replica, + £50. Entered by Fianna Fail TD Mr. R Briscoe, later to become Dublin's Lord Mayor. This same car won the Leinster Trophy driven by Miss Fay Taylour, also in 1934.

5. J F Sutherland, Singer 972cc. Finished 6th.*

6. C H Manders, Bugatti 1990cc. Retired following an ill-judged attack on the steps of the monument outside the Town Hall. This straight-eight engined Type 37, had won European hillclimbs in the hands of Frenchmen Robert Benoist and Albert Divo.

7. T O'Shaughnessy, Riley 1087cc. Retired with mechanical trouble.

8. F A Gannon, Lea-Francis 1497cc. Retired with mechanical trouble.

9. W T McCalla, Sunbeam 1988cc supercharged. Finished 2nd Awarded the Joseph McGrath Cup – to be won outright + £25, and the Fruitfield Cup – to be won outright – (presented by Mr. William H Lamb) for the fastest speed for cars exceeding 1100cc. This car had previously been the property of Sir Henry Seagrave.

10. H C McFerran, Bugatti 1990cc. Crashed at Martello Bend.

11. F O'Boyle, O'Boyle-Riley 1089cc. Retired with mechanical trouble.

12. A H Verschoyle, Frazer-Nash 1496cc. Non-starter. (Driver strained his right arm during Thursday's Practice Session).

13. The number 13 was thought unlucky and was not used.

14. F. Pearson, Lea-Francis 1497cc supercharged. Finished 7th.
Car entered by Miss L Rich.

15. 'Alan Corry', MG Magna 1087cc. Retired with mechanical trouble.
Car entered by HC McFerran, drivers real name not declared.

16. C G Neill, Bugatti 1990cc. The car somersaulted three times at Montore Bend, the driver had been thrown out early during the crash. He was injured but not as seriously as was at first thought.

17. M J Hynes, Statham-Ford 3622cc. Entered by GJ Statham. Retired with mechanical trouble.

18. H D. Walsh, MG 847cc.

19. G White, MG 1250cc. Finished 3rd, Awarded the Bray Head Hotel Cup, - to be won outright - (presented by Mr. F Bethel) + £15.

20. W J Kavanagh, MG 747cc Supercharged. Non-starter. The car had been damaged the previous week in an event in London. The Bray Officials refused permission for the driver to change his car to a Riley as the date for entries had already passed when he made the request.
21. D C MacLachlan, Riley 1087cc. Finished 5th. Awarded the McGuirk Cup – to be won outright – for the fastest speed for cars under 1100cc.
22. S Spratt, Le Mans Singer 972cc. Finished 8th*. Car entered by PJ Tracy Ltd.
23. D Yule, Austin 747cc supercharged. Retired with mechanical trouble.
24. W R (Bobby) Baird, Riley 1098cc. Entered by Major William Baird,
The car was on the starting line, but the driver was suffering from a severe chill and on medical advice was a non-starter. Baird was to have been the handicap scratch man.

* Winners of the Team Prize. (Singer)
Team Award – Set of three Silver Club Medals.

Every Finisher – apart from the winners of other awards – was given a Club Exhibition Bronze Medal.

1934 race winner, RBS (Paddy) Le Fanu, is congratulated following his success by a race official.

BRAY 1935
THE ARRANGEMENTS

After the memorable day provided for all the previous year it was agreed to again hold the Round the Houses races in 1935. The traders of Bray felt that by holding the event on the Whitsun Weekend (in 1934) they had missed out on those who would normally be visiting their town for the holiday anyway. Following considerable debate the date of Saturday 18th May was chosen (Whitsun being in June that year). The event would act as a curtain-raiser for the town's Summer Season. Bray was now under the jurisdiction of a recently elected Urban District Council with whom the IMRC had to renegotiate their mandate for running the event.

The local apathy complained about the previous year had disappeared and everyone seemed interested and excited about the race. All the talk was about the appearance of the great Stanley Woods who it was rumoured would drive a 'works' Austin. Whether this was to be one of the new OHV-engined versions was never known as the entry did not materialise.

For the 1935 race, the previous year's winner, RBS Le Fanu, drove the larger-engined Adler (1900cc).

PRACTICE

As with the previous year Practice took place between 5 and 7am on the Thursday before the race. Of the twenty-seven entries twenty-two took part in the Practice Session, with twenty-one qualifying. The one car that didn't qualify was the elderly Salmson of local man WA McQuillian who suffered connecting rod problems. He made a special appeal to the Stewards of the Meeting to be allowed to race on the Saturday if he could get his car running by then. As McQuillian lived on the actual course, and knew the circuit intimately, the Stewards acceded to this request. Not that it did the unfortunate man any good, as despite being the limit man (with a handicap advantage of 10 Laps + 3 minutes and 30 seconds) in the race itself, the car only lasted two laps before suffering engine bearing failure.

Amongst the non-starters were the joint scratch-men Arthur Dobson in a 2600cc supercharged Alfa Romeo, (who had made the fastest times in both the Leinster Trophy at Skerries and the Phoenix Park Race in 1934), and Charlie Dobson in a 2300cc Supercharged Bugatti. This was a huge disappointment for the spectators, as an exciting performance had been anticipated from the brothers Dobson. Another driver missing was Dubliner 'F Sivid' who had been entered in a 1500cc rear-engined Mercedes-Benz. HC McFerran had sold his 1990cc Bugatti to W Sullivan ten days before the race. The Stewards, however, decided that as the nomination of Sullivan as driver had not been received before the date stated in the regulations, they could not permit him to start.

Those wishing to talk-up the importance of the event were keen to point out the 'international' element. Adler works mechanics had been sent over from Germany to tune the four Adlers taking part in the race – RBS Le Fanu this year driving a larger engined car of 1990cc; CHW Manders and HD Walsh driving 1645cc cars; and EM Mitchell in a 995cc model. There were also two entrants from London - GFA Manby-Colegrave's 1087cc MG Magnette and G Bagratouni's 1287cc MG Magnette, while the Ulster Automobile Club had seven drivers entered.

The Free State, as it was then known, was represented with drivers from Counties Dublin, Meath, Kilkenny, Tipperary and Wicklow.

Coming off the mile-long sea front straight, many drivers found Boat-house corner difficult to navigate. In these photograph, F O'Boyle (O'Boyle-Riley Special No 14) gets it all wrong, while PBS Le Fanu (Adler No 11) and WR Baird (MG Magnette No 5) make it around O'Boyle successfully.

For the second year of the race the distance had been lengthened from the 102 miles of 1934 to 128 miles – a total of 40 laps. Members of the newly formed Volunteer Force (in full Army Uniform) undertook the duties of course marshalling, the first time that they had been deployed in such a role.

G White (MG) spins completely around, in the process being narrowly missed by CG Neill (Bugatti).

THE LAP RECORD

The race on Saturday the 18th May started punctually at 3.30pm, the roads having been officially closed around three o'clock. For some strange reason the handicappers had given Trevor McCalla's 1922cc supercharged Sunbeam a three lap advantage (despite his performance the previous year) over the now (virtual) scratch-man GFA Manby-Colegrave in his supercharged 1087cc MG Magnette. As they were both on the same time handicap, they were flagged away from the starting line together. McCalla made the better start, but by the time they had completed their first lap the Englishman had taken over the lead.

These two drivers then set about each other in a duel for fastest lap honours, providing the spectators with a thrilling spectacle. On lap two Manby-Colegrave lowered last year's record (set by McCalla) by three seconds. Next lap McCalla responded by shaving another second off, while on lap Four, Manby-Colegrave managed to take two more seconds off. On lap seven it was McCalla again with another second off the lap record. Lap eight saw Manby-Colegrave lower the record by one more second, then on lap ten he found yet another second. In the first ten circuits of the Bray track these two drivers between them broke the lap record no less than six times, Manby-Colegrave finally leaving it at 3 minutes 19 seconds, a speed of 57.82 miles per hour. When one thinks of the number of corners, the narrowness of road in places, and indeed the handling capabilities of the cars of those days, this was truly an astonishing achievement. At this stage these two drivers who had been 'flying' were somewhat slowed as they had caught up with the slower traffic, and had to thread their way carefully through the slower cars.

HIGH NUMBER OF FINISHERS

One interesting aspect of the 1935 race was the fact that out of the twenty-two starters thirteen qualified as finishers. (Plus another three cars that were still circulating when the rule kicked-in stating that to qualify as a finisher a driver must complete the allotted distance within fifteen minutes of the winner crossing the line). The rate of attrition in 1935 was much less than it had been the previous year – improvements in mechanical reliability perhaps?

SOME DIDN'T MAKE IT

That is not to say that there were not some mechanical casualties, with F O'Boyle's 1087cc O'Boyle-Riley Special (fractured petrol pipe) and D Yule in a 747cc supercharged Austin (bearings) retiring. Pit stops were made by F Pearson 1497cc Lea Francis (oil) having pushed the car half a mile to effect repairs, (even with this extra oil on board it was only a few more laps before an enforced retirement occurred), and EM Mitchell 995cc Adler (gearbox) who did get going again.

The only incidents reported were to GE White whose 1246 MG Magna overturned at Town Hall Hairpin, fortunately without harm to the driver, and McCalla hitting a dog that had unwisely strayed onto Seafront Road. The poor dog was killed, but no damage appears to have been caused to the Sunbeam, although it's racing line through Boathouse Corner was most certainly altered in a big way that lap.

The duel between G Manby-Colgrave (MG Magnette s/c No 3) and WT McCalla (Sunbeam s/c No 4) to set the fastest lap kept the crowds enthralled for much of the early part of the race.

Leaving the starting line. WR Baird (MG Magnette No 5) and P Dwyer (Bugatti No 10) get away. The Pits, complete with paper streamers, can be seen in the background.

THE IRISH WEATHER

At the start the sun had shone gloriously, and the biting wind of the previous day had died down to a gentle breeze. Although at times it looked threatening, rain did not fall until well into the race. Then suddenly, the breeze turned into a squall of extreme violence, dislodging the advertising signs and streamers decorating the pits, tearing them to pieces and scattering them across the course. Race officials were seen dashing in and out between the competing cars to retrieve these papers, how nobody was injured remains a mystery. The rain then came down in torrents, drenching officials, spectators & drivers indiscriminately. While these conditions only lasted for ten minutes, and subsided as suddenly as they had arrived, it did leave the roadway very wet, which favoured the slower cars.

Manby-Colegrave and McCalla had been working their way steadily through the slower cars, but their progress was now somewhat halted, indeed, both called to the pits for visors because of the level of spray they were having to contend with.

The aftermath of the torrential rain can be seen as T O'Shaughnessy (Riley No 9), followed by MJ Hynes (Statham-Ford Special No 8) splash under the railway bridge on Seapoint Road.

THE RACE LEADERS

Up front the high-handicappers were indulging in place swapping throughout the race with names on the leader board being changed nearly every lap due to overtaking, or mechanical problems. Suddenly, fortunes were completely changed, with Manby-Colegrave forced into retirement with valve problems, and McCalla, who had worked his way up to third place and was gaining on the two cars ahead of him, developing a severe mis-fire. A quick call at his pits failed to cure the problem (later to be traced to cotton-wool in the fuel line) and he limped around the track for the rest of the race, being very fortunate to finish in sixth place.

As the race progressed, first it was D Yule's 747cc supercharged Austin, then 'D Squires' in a 1246cc MG Magna, and later FA Gannon's 1497cc Lea Francis that held the lead. Then, on the penultimate lap DM McCracken driving Ainsley Verschoyle's 1496cc Frazer Nash swept to the front, having reeled in the various cars in front of him with a steady and determined drive. And so the race finished with Trinity Law Student Desmond McCracken taking the spoils in what was his first ever race, by eight seconds from Frank Gannon, with Paddy Le Fanu a further 2 mins. 43 secs. back in third place.

THE CELEBRATIONS

As with the previous year the day's festivities ended with a dance and prize distribution held in the Opera Hall of Woodbrook Golf Club, which was attended by race officials, drivers, and many of Bray's civic and business leaders. The cost of attending this function was eight shillings. The dancing continuing late into the night, with the mood of the evening being described as "full of mirth and gaiety".

D Yule (Austin s/c No 27) is followed around Billow corner by eventual race winner DM McCracken (Frazer-Nash No 16).

A HARSH DECISION

The press release which was widely reported in the newspapers stated that the winners of the Team Award were the Ulster Automobile Club Team of WT McCalla (Sunbeam), 'D. Squires' (MG Magna), and CG Neill (Bugatti), but following a meeting of the Stewards after the race, the prize was never presented. It transpired that Neill (6) with one lap still to complete was approaching the finishing line in company with G Bagratouni (9) who had completed his full distance. A race official held the card showing the number 9 upside-down. Neill, thinking that he had completed his race, simply toured around. When he eventually arrived back at his pit, the official responsible, having been made aware of his mistake, made frantic signals to get Neill to again cross the finishing line. However, by this time Neill was outside the time limit (15 minutes after the winner crosses the line) by a mere thirteen seconds, thus preventing him from qualifying as a finisher.

Winner DM McCracken (Frazer-Nash No 16) receives the adulation of the crowd.

DRIVING INCOGNITO

Two names appearing in the Official Programme as drivers 'D. Squires' and 'L. Ripley' turned out to be FD Maguire and HW Furney respectively. To enter under a false name was quite a common practice at the time, for many and various reasons.

SAD FATE

It is sad to report that some weeks after the 1935 Bray event second-placed man Frank Austin Gannon was killed in an accident involving a motor-cyclist at Templeogue, County Dublin, when he and a friend were returning from carrying out a 'recce' of the proposed Tallaght course. Irish motor sport lost a talented and popular figure that day.

One of the eventual winner DM McCracken's (Frazer-Nash No 16) handicap laps is about to disappear as he is caught by the very fast pair of G Manby-Colgrave (MG Magnette s/c No 3) and WT McCalla (Sunbeam s/c No 4).

FUTURE OF THE RACE

In the two years that the round the houses races were held in Bray it was obvious that the road surface along Strand Road was deteriorating in a dangerous manner and this situation was not helped by a harsh winter in 1935. So, a decision regarding improvements had to be made for safety reasons before any further motor sport participation could be considered. Unfortunately, the road authorities of the day did not have sufficient finances to undertake an improvement scheme of this magnitude, and therefore despite the success of the events held in 1934 and 1935, this was to be the end of motor racing of that type in this splendid seaside town. Interestingly, a report in *The Wicklow People* newspaper during 1946 of a meeting of the Bray Town Council showed that a discussion had taken place about the possibilities of reviving the Round the Houses races. However, due to the costs involved and the disruption that would be caused to the local citizenry the idea was abandoned.

DON'T FORGET THE
CAR RACE DANCE
will be held in
THE OPERA HALL, WOODBROOK.
ON THIS (SATURDAY) NIGHT.
Dancing 9 to 2 :: Evening Dress.
RED TIGERS BAND.
TICKETS - - - - 5/- (including Tax).
Parking Accommodation. Buffet and Bar.
Car Race Trophies will be presented at the Dance.

The Irish Motor Racing Club didn't neglect the social side of motor racing.

1935 RACE RESULTS

A fine shot of eventual 1935 winner DM McCracken (Frazer-Nash No 16) at speed during the race.

Position	*Driver*	*Car*	*H*	*M*	*S*	*MPH*
1st	DM McCracken	1496 Frazer Nash	2	10	14	51.24
2nd	FA Gannon	1497 Lea Francis	2	10	22	47.98
3rd	RBS Le Fanu	1990 Adler	2	12	57	51.85
4th	MJ Hynes	3633 Statham-Ford	2	15	24	51.54
5th	'D. Squires'	1246 MG Magna	2	15	35	45.42
6th	WT McCalla	1992 Sunbeam s/c	2	16	30	52.36
7th	WR Baird	1287 MG Magnette s/c	2	16	38	52.11
8th	'L. Ripley'	1287 MG Magnette	2	17	18	46.94
9th	P. Dwyer	3255 Bugatti	2	17	33	50.37
10th	WJ Kavanagh	1287 MG Magnette	2	17	47	48.19
11th	G Bagratouni	1287 MG Magnette	2	19	05	50.17
12th	T O'Shaughnessy	1087 Riley	2	20	15	45.93
13th	EM Mitchell	995 Adler	2	22	11	44.50

THE AWARDS

The Earl of Meath's Perpetual Trophy + £50 – Winner of the race,
DH McCracken, Dublin, Frazer Nash.
The Walsh Cup + £30 – FA Gannon, Meath, Lea Francis.
The O'Neill Cup + £20 – RBS Le Fanu, Bray, Adler.

All those who completed the course were awarded Club silver plaques.

(The money for the second and third prizes was provided by two bookmakers, Billy Walsh of Shankill and W O'Neill of Bray.)

ADLER

ACHIEVEMENTS

BRAY ROUND THE HOUSES. **1st.** Mr. R. B. S. Le Fanu, driving standard **Adler Trumpf.** Speed 45.5 m.p.h.

LEINSTER TROPHY RACE. **1st.** Miss Fay Taylour, driving standard **Adler Trumpf.** Speed 61.20 m.p.h.

Now ! 13 International Class G. Records with **Adler Junior** at Avus Track, Berlin

4,000 kms.	48 hours.
3,000 miles.	72 hours.
5,000 kms.	96 hours.
4,000 miles.	120 hours.
5,000 miles.	144 hours.
10,000 kms.	
15,000 kms.	

10,000 miles at 66.01 m.p.h. Improving previous record by 52hrs. 48min. 27sec.

ADLER JUNIOR 10.5 H.P. ... £275.

Sole Distributors:

Irish Exporters & Importers, Ltd

16 UPPER MAYOR STREET, DUBLIN.

The Irish importers of Adler cars extensively advertised the success of their cars in the 1934 Bray and Skerries races

The Riley of T O'Shaughnessy leads the Statham-Ford Special of MJ Hynes in the 1934 race while the Adler of eventual winner, RBS le Fanu comes up behind.

OFFICIALS OF THE 1934 AND 1935 CUAIRT BHRE CAR RACES

Stewards of the Meetings: PS Brady, Irish Motor Racing Club (1934/35)
Capt. RD Greer, Royal Irish Automobile Club (1934/35)
Capt. WJ Thompson, Ulster Automobile Club (1934/35)

Clerk of the Course AND Secretary of the Meeting: Major Niall MacNeill (1934/35)

Chief Marshal: Major Niall MacNeill (1934). Barry Egan (1935)

Assistant Chief Marshals:
CJ Walsh. Barry Egan, A Robinson, J Gordon Burney, DP Harris (1934)
PL MacDonnell, PD O'Grady, J Gordon Burney, DP Harris, FW Harrison (1935).

Assistant Secretary of the Meeting: DJ Scannell (1934/35)

Treasurer of the Meeting: A Harrison (1934/35)

Chief Technical Officer and Scrutineer (Chief Pit Marshal): ST Robinson (1934/35)

Chief Paddock Marshal: J.J. Reddy (1934). B. Redmond (1935)

Chief Timekeeper: Harold C Brown (1934). RH Wright (1935).

Chief Flag Marshal: JJ O'Neill (1934/35)

Course Engineer: EM Murphy, BE (1934/35)

Clerk of Works: IE Gibson (1934)

Chief Salvage Marshal: J Schworer (1935)

Press Secretary: Miss AM Hawe (1934)

Announcer: Capt. LM Fuge (1934)

Broadcast Commentator:
FM Summerfield (1934/35) DEH Hamilton (1935)

Chief Medical Officer: Dr. H Raverty (1934/35)

Medical Officers: Dr. AT McKay (1934/35). Dr. JF O'Grady (1934/35). Dr. C Moore (1934). Dr. John Eustace (1934/35). Dr. RB Shaw (1934). Dr. W Taylor (1934/35). Dr. McSorley (1934). Dr. Broderick (1934/35). Dr. D Reddin (1935). Dr. Leyland (1935).

The St. John's Ambulance Brigade, Under Assistant Commissioner:
AJ McWilliam (1934/35)

Judges: WH Freeman (1934/35). HG Tyrell Smith (1934/35). Dene Allen (1934). WGE Longworth (1935).

CUAIRT BHRE CAR RACE COMMITTEES

President: PJ Meghen, BE., B.Sc. (Commissioner administering the affairs of the Bray Urban District Council) (1934), E Byrne, PC. (1935).
Chairman and Hon. Treasurer: Sean McCathmhaoil, Town Clerk (1934/35).
Hon. Secretaries: P Devitt (1934/35). JR Lindsay (1934).
Committee: Right Hon. Earl of Meath (1934). Rev. FA Gleeson C.C. (1934). Rev. Austin MA. (1934). Major Niall MacNeill (1934). The O'Mahony TD (1934). Dr. H Raverty MB. (1934/35). FB Jameson (1934). Dr. W Taylor (1934). CHW Manders (1934). HC Brown (1934). EM Murphy BE. (34/35). F Bethel (1934).TW Murphy (1934). W Poole (1934). FM Summerfield (1934). JJ Reddy (1934). PJ Scraggs (1934). Frame (1934/35). PH McCarthy BE. (1934). E Scott (1934). O Tansey (1934/35). J Duffy PC. (1934/35).JH Cahill (1934). MM Doyle (1934). JP Tyrell Solicitor (1934/35). MJ Hoey (1934). W Browne (1934). J Byrne (1934). D Frame Jr. (1934). JB Dawson (1934). C Haig (1934). Right Hon. Viscount Powerscourt (1934). Colonel E Broy (1934). Chief Supt. O'Carroll (1934). Supt. O'Reilly (1934/35). S Moore TD (1934). J Everett TD (1934). W Twoomey BL. (1934). CR Lurring (1934/35). CJ Walsh (1934). A Harrison (1934). SG Gallagher BE. (1934). CH Murphy (1934). ST Robinson (1934). A Doyle (1934). John O'Neill (1934). S Hutchinson (1934/35). PJ.Byrne (1934). JJ Doyle (1934/35). O Trainor (1934). E Byrne PC. (1934/35). J Cleary (1934). J O'Brien (1934). B Rusk (34/35). G Cooper (1934).
E Jordan Solicitor (1934/35). PL MacDonnell (1934). CR Lochner (1934/35). PJ Sexton (1934). J McGuirk (1934). DJ Mackey (1934). O. Tansey (1935). Inspector Murphy (1935). Mrs. O'Gorman (1935). EM Murphy BE. (1935). EJ MacDonnell (1935). CJ Davidson (1935)

VF Ross (Jowett Jupiter) crossing the finish line in the MG Car Club's Sprint meeting on the Bray Promenade in September 1951.

MG CAR CLUB SPRINT – SEPTEMBER 1st 1951

Having decided in 1946 that to revive the Round-the-Houses racing would be too expensive & disruptive, the Urban District Council were approached and gave their approval to the MG Car Club (Irish Centre) to hold a Sprint along a half mile section of the Esplanade on Saturday 1st September 1951. As far as can be ascertained this was the first motor sport event to be held in Bray since 1935.

The event attracted a reasonable entry with a variety of machinery, in fact everything from powerful Jaguar's to lowly 'Specials'. These Specials or 'Bitza' (bits of this & bits of that) were a common feature of motor sport in the years following the Second World War, and consisted of home constructed vehicles, some competitive - some not. A lot used the chassis of a pre-war car with the original body removed and an open single or two seat (usually light weight) body built in its place. Ford were a great source for this purpose, but by no means the only marque to donate!

Weather on the day was fine and dry, while the *Wicklow People* reported a huge crowd in attendance. Among the non-starters were Joe Kelly who was to drive both his Irish Racing Auto (another home built Special) and his GP Alta, while Redmond Gallagher had been entered to drive his 966cc JAP engined Leprechaun.

The Sprint allowed a driver to use more than one car, or for two drivers to share a car, for example:- Cecil Vard drove both his Jaguar XK 120 (in which he recorded Best Time of the Day) and the Jaguar Mark 5 saloon in which he had gained third place in that year's Monte Carlo Rally. While Dick Lovell-Butt shared the driving of his very fast supercharged monoposto MG Magnette with popular and energetic MG Car Club secretary Shelia O'Clery, who was making her debut in a speed event.

Also on his first car event was motor-cyclist Tony Jacobs, probably better know as skipper of the famous little ship *Ituna* which had recently made a gallant and successful crossing of the Atlantic from Dublin to New York. Tony was rewarded for his efforts in the Jaguar XK 120 with third best time in the open scratch class.

Back to those 'Special's' again, noted for their fast performance were:- Irwin Catherwood's Bugatti-Ford, (while the Ford V8 engine made hardly a sound, there was a high-pitched whine from its straight tooth Bugatti rear axle) coming 4th in the open scratch class. Meanwhile a mere 0.4 seconds slower in that class was the Trifor (Mercury engined, Triumph chassis) of Alec Macarthur.

Fastest of the T-type MG's was Nat Preston driving his unblown TC. Lady drivers were successfully represented by Mrs. D L Bigger driving her MG Y-type saloon, and Miss Anita Newell driving her brother's famous old racing 12/50 Alvis (despite this car having a troublesome pre-selector gearbox).

This was the first opportunity for the public to see Irish assembled Volkswagen Beetle's in competitive action, and they were not to be disappointed.

RESULTS

Best Time of Day:	C Vard (XK 120 Jaguar) 22.99 secs. (64.07 mph)	
2nd Fastest:	RG Lovell-Butt (1,087 MG S/c) 23.78 secs.	
Open Handicap:	1. JC Millard (1,250 MG);	2. NE Gleeson (VW).
1,250cc Handicap:	1. JC Millard (MG);	2. PJ Van Miest (MG).
Over 1,250 Handicap:	1. Miss A Newell (Alvis).	
Open MG Handicap:	JC Millard.	
Saloon MG Handicap:	Mrs. DL Biggeer.	
Ladies Class Handicap:	Miss A Newell (Alvis).	
1,250 cc Scratch:	JN Preston (MG).	
1500 cc Scratch:	MP Cahill (Iona Special).	
3,000 cc Unsupercharged & 1,500 cc Supercharged Scratch:	RG Lovell-Butt (MG).	
Open Scratch:	1. C Vard (Jaguar); 3. ACB Jacobs (Jaguar).	2. RG Lovell-Butt (MG);

INDEX OF DRIVERS

The following is the list of drivers officially entered in the Bray races in 1934 and 1935.
A more detailed list of results for the 1934 race appears earlier in this Album.

Driver	*Years*	*Race Number*	*Make*	*Result*
G Bagratouni	1935	9	MG Magnette	11th
WR Baird	1934	24	Riley 1098cc	N/S
	1935	5	MG Magnette	7th
'A Corry'	1934	15	MG Magna1087cc	Rtd.
A Dobson	1935	1	Alfa-Romeo s/c	N/S
AC Dobson	1935	2	Bugatti	N/S
P Dwyer	1935	10	Bugatti	9th
FA Gannon	1934	8	Lea-Francis 1497cc	Rtd.
	1935	22	Lea-Francis 1487cc	2nd
MJ Hynes	1934	17	Statham-Ford Spl.3622cc	Rtd.
	1935	8	Statham-Ford Spl.3622cc	4th
WJ Kavanagh	1934	20	MG s/c 747cc	N/S
	1935	17	MG Magnette	10th
RBS Le Fanu	1934	4	Adler 1994 cc	1st
	1935	11	Adler 1990cc	3rd
WT McCalla	1934	9	Sunbeam s/c 1988cc	2nd
	1935	4	Sunbeam s/c 1988cc	6th
DM McCracken	1935	16	Frazer-Nash	1st
HC McFerran	1934	10	Bugatti 1990cc	Crashed
	1935	7	Bugatti 1990cc	Rtd.
J McGrattan	1935	25	MG Midget	N/S
DC MacLachlan	1934	21	Riley 1087cc	5th
D McMullan	1934	2	MG Magnette 1287cc	Rtd.
WA McQuillan	1935	28	Salmson	Rtd.
G Nanby-Colegrave	1935	3	MG Magnette s/c	Rtd.
CH Manders	1934	6	Bugatti 1990cc	Rtd.
	1935	12	Adler	Rtd.
EM Mitchell	1935	20	Adler	13th
CG Neill	1934	16	Bugatti	Crashed
	1935	6	Bugatti	Rtd.

Driver	*Years*	*Race Number*	*Make*	*Result*
F O'Boyle	1934	11	O'Boyle-Riley Spl.	Rtd.
	1935	14	O'Boyle-Riley Spl.	Rtd.
T O'Shaughnessy	1934	7	Riley	Rtd.
	1935	19	Riley	12th
F Pearson	1934	14	Lea-Francis s/c	7th
	1935	26	Lea-Francis	Rtd.
'L Ripley'	1935	18	MG Magnette	8th
'F Sivad'	1935	21	Mercedes-Benz	N/S
S Spratt	1934	22	Le Mans Singer 972cc	8th
'D Squires'	1935	25	MG Magna	5th
JF Sutherland	1934	5	Singer 972cc	6th
CW Taylor	1934	1	Le Mans Singer 972cc	4th
HD Walsh	1934	18	MG 847cc	Rtd.
	1935	15	Adler	Rtd.
G White	1934	19	MG 1250cc	3rd
	1935	23	MG Magna	Rtd.
CH Wilson	1934	3	Vauxhall	Rtd.
AH Verschoyle	1934	12	Frazer-Nash 1496cc	N/S
D Yule	1934	23	Austin s/c 747cc	Rtd.
	1935	27	Austin s/c	Rtd.

The Ulster Automobile Club Team. From left: W Noble (Chairman of the UAC); WT McCalla (Sunbeam No 4); WR Baird (MG MagnetteNo 5); CB Neill (Bugatti No 6); 'L Ripley' (MG Magnette No 18) and 'D Squires' (MG Magna No 24), who, driving under an assumed name, ensured that his identity would not be revealed in photographs either!

THE GUINNESS SEGRAVE LIBRARY AND ARCHIVE OF THE ROYAL IRISH AUTOMOBILE CLUB

The RIAC Guinness Segrave Library and Archive was established by Wilford J Fitzsimmons in 1985 with the generous support of the 3rd Earl of Iveagh. The Library commemorates two members of the Guinness family, Sir Algernon and his brother Kenelm Lee, who together with their contemporary, Sir Henry Segrave, were amongst the first Irish drivers to carve out an international reputation for themselves in the exacting world of motor sport.

The Library contains many rare volumes including 'runs' of Mecredy's *Irish Cyclist* and *Motor News*. That other early Irish journal, *The Irish Wheelman,* is also well represented within the Library, which also contains 'runs' of the more usual journals of record, *The Autocar, The Motor, Motor Sport, Speed* and of more recent times, *Autosport*. As such, the RIAC Guinness Segrave Library is an important collection of motoring literature, while its material relating to early Irish motoring is quite unique, and because Ireland took centre stage in the world of motorsport at the time of the 1903 Gordon Bennett Race, the Irish International Grand Prix series from 1929-31 and during the golden age of the Tourist Trophy series from 1928-1936, its value as an important motoring archive is greatly enhanced.

Since 1985 the Library has continued to grow through further gifts of motoring literature and its collection of photographs, programmes and other motoring memorabilia has reached the stage where this now forms an important archive in itself. The Library is not open to the public but access is given to bone-fide researchers through the RIAC's Archive Curator. It is hoped to develop further the Dreoilín series of Transport Albums, in association with the Archive, to extend over a wide range of transport related subjects of Irish interest.

The Archive Group also includes the popular Double 20 Club for competitors who held a competition licence forty or more years ago.

If you would like to assist the Archive's work of preserving Ireland's unique motoring heritage, why not join the 'Friends of the Archive Group' – details from:
The Curator, RIAC Archive, 34 Dawson Street, Dublin 2.

THE AUTHOR

Robin McCullagh is a past President of both the Irish Veteran & Vintage Car Club and the MG Enthusiasts Club. He has been interested and involved in cars from an early age. Robin previously produced books for the MG Enthusiasts Club's 21st Anniversary and the Motor Enthusiasts Club 50th Anniversary. Being always fascinated with the idea of round-the houses Motor Racing meant that research for the Bray events was a particular pleasure.

ACKNOWLEDGEMENTS

In carrying out research into the Bray Round the Houses motor races, I am most grateful to the following organisations and people for assistance:

The Irish Times, The Wicklow People, The National Library of Ireland, *The Daily Express,* Bray Library (Robert Butler) and Wicklow County Library (Ciara Brennan).

The Royal Irish Automobile Club Archive, who provided: *The History of Motorsport in Ireland 1903-1969* by W.A. McMaster; *Green Dust* by Brendan Lynch; the *Irish Motor News; The Ulster Automobile Club Monthly Review; Bray Historical Record Volume 1 Number 8.*

Henry Cairns of Bray Town Hall Bookshop, who provided wise counsel and copies of his books *Pictorial History of Bray*. Also Ray Cowen, Norman Colin, Tom Farrell, Bob Montgomery, Dr. David McCullagh, Jim Scannell and Mrs. Bobby Smith.

Published by Dreoilín Specialist Publications Limited,
Tankardstown, Garristown, County Meath, Ireland.

Trade enquiries to Argosy Books
Telephone (00353) 1 8239500

First published in 2010

ISBN 978-1-902773-20-9

A CIP record for this title is available from the British Library

Designed and set in 9 point Times Roman by Alan Pepper Design, and printed in the Republic of Ireland by Walsh Colour Print.